FISH TALES
Text copyright © 2001 by Steve Chapman.
Artwork © 2007 by James, Robert, and Joseph Hautman, collectively
The Hautman Brothers. Courtesy of MHS Licensing.

Published by Harvest House Publishers
Eugene, Oregon 97402
ISBN-13: 978-0-7369-1850-3
ISBN-10: 0-7369-1850-7

Design and production by Koechel Peterson & Associates, Minneapolis, MN

Portions of this text are excerpted from *Reel Time with God* by Steve Chapman
(Harvest House Publishers, 2001).

Printed in Hong Kong

07 08 09 10 11 12 13 14 15 / NG / 10 9 8 7 6 5 4 3 2 1

The traveler fancies he has seen the country.
So he has, the outside of it at least; but the angler only sees the inside.
The angler only is brought close, face to face with the flower
and bird and insect life of the rich river banks, the only part
of the landscape where the hand of man has never interfered.

CHARLES KINGSLEY

Hooked from the Start

All Americans believe that they are born fishermen.

For a man to admit a distaste for fishing

would be like denouncing mother-love or hating moonlight.

JOHN STEINBECK

One of my most valued possessions is a black-and-white photo taken in 1956. It's one of those things I hope I have time to grab if I am suddenly forced to escape a house fire. It speaks of a day I will forever cherish, and to lose that picture would be a personal tragedy.

What's in the snapshot? It's me as a little boy standing on the muddy bank of a small farm pond in West Virginia behind the country home of Robert and Rose Duty. In one hand is a cane fishing pole and in the other is the thin line. Hanging on the hook is my very first fish, a tiny bluegill! My smile of excitement is obvious but not huge. I seem happy about catching something but scared of what I held hostage. It appears as though I wondered, "This is really neat, but what do I do now?" Like a bookmark in the pages of my past, this black-and-white treasure is a testimony of my introduction to the world of angling.

A first fish, like the one I caught, is more than a floppy, slimy, smelly slab of scales and fins. It represents the gift of time spent in the great outdoors. The appearance of a fish on the line is a priceless treasure children can hold on to. As a result of the excitement of feeling the tug and pull of landing that initial fish, children can get hooked on an activity that can eventually encourage them to discover similar opportunities for spending time with their own kids!

It only took a couple of trips to the water with my little kids and fishing gear for me to realize, "If you want to be with your kids, take them fishing... but if you want to go fishing, don't take the kids." The sacrifice of much-needed solitude (and safety as well, since those wildly flying hooks on a child's line can hurt a fellow) was worth the return I experienced. As a result of catching their first fish with Dad standing by, I have two grown children who are my friends as much as they are my offspring. Our closeness has value beyond measure because it meets an incredibly important need—time spent together in love!

If people concentrated on the really important things in life, there'd be a shortage of fishing poles.

DOUG LARSON

Of Flies and Men

Humans and frogs have at least two things in common: fun and flies. We say, "Time flies when you're having fun." They say, "Time's fun when you're having flies!" Thankfully, they have been chosen to consume the disgusting insects. For us, unless we are yawning on a fast-moving motorcycle, we are privileged to find joy in using flies. We humans who fish can feed the appetites of our adventurer hearts by throwing out fake flies with lines and leaders and rods.

MORE THAN HALF THE INTENSE ENJOYMENT OF FLY-FISHING IS DERIVED FROM THE BEAUTIFUL SURROUNDINGS, THE SATISFACTION FELT FROM BEING IN THE OPEN AIR, THE NEW LEASE OF LIFE SECURED THEREBY, AND THE MANY, MANY PLEASANT RECOLLECTIONS OF ALL ONE HAS SEEN, HEARD, AND DONE.

CHARLES F. ORVIS

There's something very satisfying and restful about gently and accurately laying a chosen bait on the surface of a slow-moving pool. That alone is plenty of reward. Add the sudden explosion of water and the exciting pull of the line, and you have the necessary ingredients to make the icing that goes on the adrenaline cake.

Stepping down off a bank into the cold, uneven bed of a trout stream and feeling the weight of the water press my rubber waders against my legs is a step of bliss for me. And how often it is needed! Getting away from the phone, fax machines, the Internet, and the busy streets filled with exhaust fumes creates a precious time. Sometimes a fellow just needs it. Occasionally a person has to put the brakes on and take a breather before he or she breaks! If not, a mind can snap like 10-pound test line being yanked by a 90-pound striped bass!

All fishermen will appreciate Psalm 23:2-3. The passage was custom written for them: "He makes me lie down in green pastures [taking a break from fishing and having lunch]; He leads me beside quiet waters [Yes! Back to fishing]. He restores my soul [Caught one!]."

Why is this psalm so important? Here's one reason: Unlike frogs, who know how to sit motionless for long periods of time in order to outsmart a skittish insect, most humans do not naturally embrace the skill of resting. We so easily yield to the temptation of being overactive. The balance between work and rest has been sadly lost.

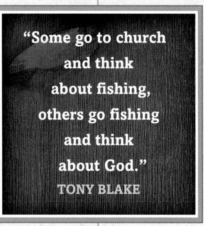

"Some go to church and think about fishing, others go fishing and think about God."
TONY BLAKE

It is important to take note that a primary word in the definition of "restores" is "rest." We can take a valuable lesson from our little green friends. We would do well to be content, at least every once in a while, with ceasing from our labors. Everyone needs the benefits of taking a break by having fun. May you see the fun in stopping for a while to have . . . that is . . . to cast some flies.

I now believe that fishing
is far more important
than the fish.
ARNOLD GINGRICH

My Pa he ist fished an' fished!
An' my Ma she said she wished
Me an' her was home; an' Pa
Said he wished so worse'n Ma.

Pa said ef you talk, er say
Anything, er sneeze, er play,
Hain't no fish, alive er dead,
Ever go' to bit! he said.

Purt' nigh dark in town when we
Got back home; an' Ma says she,
Now she'll have a fish fer shore!
An' she buyed one at the store.

Nen at supper, Pa he won't
Eat no fish, an' says he don't
Like 'em.—An' he pounded me
When I choked!...Ma, didn't he?

JAMES WHITCOMB RILEY

from *The Fishing Party*

While he hears in every spring

How the birds do chirp and sing:

Or before the hounds in cry

See the hare go stealing by:

Or along the shallow brook,

Angling with a baited hook,

See the fishes leap and play

In a blessed sunny day.

NICHOLAS BRETON

"Who Can Live in Heart So Glad"

Good fishing never stops.
There are only times when in some places
it is better than others.

George Fichter

I stand up and can feel that mild,

aching joy of the first fish as I look to

the long river moss in the crystal gravel channels,

streaming and wavering like radio signals.

Thomas McGuane
from *The Longest Silence*

There are always greater fish
than you have caught,
always the lure of greater task and achievement,
always the inspiration to seek,
to endure, to find.

ZANE GRAY

James Hautman

Faith OF THE Fisherman

I AM A MAN WHO passionately loves the outdoors. If I had a choice between eating a scrumptious, expensive meal inside a big city restaurant or sitting on a creek bank with half a peanut butter sandwich, I would opt for a little bite of food and a big piece of the sky. While my admitted obsession with being "out there" might be better than other vices, an unbridled affection for enjoying nature has its drawbacks. One particularly negative side effect is often revealed in my heart when a springtime Sunday morning rolls around.

Here in our neck of the planet, crappie fishing season gets underway when the air starts to warm—sometime in April or May. Making an early-morning stop at the local bait shop to buy two- or three-dozen minnows, a few fresh, colorful jigs, and filling the thermos with some hot coffee to wash down the donuts is a pleasure beyond description. Mornings like that are one of the main ingredients God uses to draw us closer to Him and His creation.

While it is difficult on any day of the week to wake up and not head to the lake, it is especially hard on Sunday mornings. Being one who believes firmly it is God who formed the outdoors that we enjoy, I am also convinced I should devote time to celebrating the Creator behind the creation. As I leave my driveway and turn toward the church instead of the lake, the battle in my heart begins.

As I head down the highway, I pass pickups pulling trailers loaded with boats. Sticking up just above the railing of those fiberglass and aluminum shrines I see the bouncing tips of rods ready for reeling. I can't see them, but I know on the floors of those vessels there are coolers filled with canned drinks and snacks waiting to be consumed with a smile. The thought of it hurts. I'm almost offended that the owners of the boats take a route that taunts me with the temptation to turn around and follow them. How rude!

As the anglers go by, I look into their faces. Don't they know their smiles disturb my piety? Can't they see how anxious I am at the thought that they will be catching fish that won't be there for me to hook on Monday morning? What's wrong with these people?

God's silence says much more than I want to hear.

Even as I struggle emotionally when watching others make their way merrily to the lake, I know that ahead of me, inside the sanctuary, is the joy of obedience. And that, my friend, is a good catch!

> **MANY MEN GO FISHING
> ALL OF THEIR LIVES
> WITHOUT KNOWING
> THAT IT IS NOT FISH THEY ARE AFTER.**
>
> HENRY DAVID THOREAU

*There he stands, draped in more
equipment than a telephone lineman,
trying to outwit an organism with a brain
no bigger than a breadcrumb,
and getting licked in the process.*

PAUL O'NEIL

Reel Temptations

I can't stand it any longer. I have to try. I know no one will see me do it under the cover of darkness." I was mumbling these words to myself the night I gave in and walked through the darkness to fish in the pond behind the house where we lived years ago. When we first looked at the place to consider buying it, I noticed the small lake that graced the community. It was fenced off, and I learned from the real estate agent that it was for a good reason. The folks who owned it did not want young children playing around the water because of the legal ramifications of an accident or even a drowning.

The scuttlebutt from the neighbors was that the pond owners were vigilant about guarding their property and that absolutely no trespassing was allowed. Because of that report, I never asked to fish in the pond, assuming the answer would be a firm *no*.

In the two years I had lived at this location, I didn't see one soul drop a line into the pond. It pained me that due to such tight security around it, a grand opportunity for fishing was being unnecessarily squandered. The ache to find out what size bass or catfish might have been there for the catching grew worse every time I mowed the yard, raked the leaves, washed the car, or played with the kids in the back of the house. It tortured me to look at it. Then one evening as the sun was setting, an idea came to me as I sipped a cup of coffee on our deck and listened to the gurgling spring pouring into the far end of the one acre lake.

Waiting until the night sky was completely black and the area around the pond was dark as coal, I quietly gathered my rod and reel and headed to the backyard. With the stealth of a fox, I found my way to the fence at the edge of the pond. The only thing that separated me from the edge of the water was about six feet of nicely mowed grass. I knew all I had to do after casting the lure was to be careful not to tangle up in the chain link fence.

The two-inch strip of raw bacon from our refrigerator that hung on my hook lightly splashed when it fell into the deep end of the pool. I let it sink a little and then tightened the line. With one eye on the house above the opposite bank I held the rod in my hand and waited for a strike. I would like to tell you that something immediately hit my hook and nearly ripped the rod out of my hands. I wish I could say that my suspicions that the pond was filled to the brim with trophy fish begging to be caught were proven true. But nothing happened.

In the actionless three or four minutes that I waited for a bite, something inside me began to grow more and more uncomfortable. I felt like I was being watched. I checked all around me but saw no movement and heard no stirring. While I was sure I was fishing unseen, there was a gnawing awareness that I was already caught. And then it hit me.

I had gotten so involved in the attempt to test the lake with my bait that one important truth was ignored. I realized I was feeling guilty because God was watching. Surprise! Guess who was caught at the pond!

With the tail of my ego tucked under me I headed back to the garage and put my gear away.

The minnow cost eighteenpence. It was a beautiful quill minnow, and the tackle-maker said that it could be thrown as a fly. He guaranteed further in respect to the triangles— it glittered with triangles—that, if necessary, the minnow would hold a horse. A man who speaks too much truth is just as offensive as a man who speaks too little. None the less, owing to the defective condition of the present law of libel, the tackle-maker's name must be withheld.

RUDYARD KIPLING

in *Classic Fishing Stories,* Nick Lyons, ed.

Catching Trouble

I ONLY WANTED TO SEE if I could pester the slithery intruder as it wiggled its way past my boat. The snake was about 30 yards off my starboard side and, from my aft perch, I could see it was probably about four feet long. The open-face reel neatly and quietly unraveled the line as my bait flew over the snake and dived into the water. It had landed just inches beyond the critter. When the line settled on the lake it fell right onto the snake's back. It slowed as I began to gently reel in.

I'm not quite sure how I managed to do it but the treble hook on my lure snagged the target and the next thing I knew my rod tip bent sharply down and I had myself a situation. The catch and release method of fishing sure started looking like a good idea. However, try as I would, I could not separate my unwanted guest from my hook.

I decided to reel him in closer to the boat and try using my oar to knock him off the expensive lure which was too valuable to lose. When it was within a few feet of my hull I lifted the slimy thing out of the water and held it out at rod's length. He writhed wildly in protest.

Thinking I might be able to sling the thing off, I decided to attempt a cast. It would save me from having to dig for the oar. As I brought the rod and reel over the boat to get into a casting position, the inevitable happened. The snake fell off my hook and right into the middle of the boat!

Needless to say, I headed for the highest point of my rig, the swivel seat behind me. I had no idea what kind of snake I had inadvertently invited on board, but I knew things were getting serious.

As the bewildered creature searched for cover, I went for the oar. Beating it to death was not my preference, but I was more than willing to have a change of heart. Then I remembered my hook. I thought, Why not resnag him and try lifting him out of the boat?

At this point I was very open to forfeiting my lure and feeling safe again.

So that's what I did. With hopes of not snagging the carpet, I placed the lure over the snake's back and gave it a jerk. Yes! It was hooked. With that accomplished I lifted him out of the boat, dropped him into the water, and quickly cut the line. Somewhere today there is a snake slithering around the lake with a colorful ornament permanently stuck in its side. I hope its friends are impressed!

I learned a big lesson that day. Toying with a serpent is not a wise thing to do. Next time I see one invading my space, I'll just watch it from afar.

Miss Watson she took me in the closet and prayed,
but nothing come of it. She told me to pray every day,
and whatever I asked for I would get it. But it warn't
so. I tried it. Once I got a fish-line, but no hooks.
It warn't any good to me without hooks.

Huck Finn in *The Adventures of Huckleberry Finn*
by Mark Twain

James Hautman

An Angler's Ingenuity

When I was much younger, the little bells that hung around the necks of stuffed toys and were found on the strings of baby's shoes had great value to those of us who enjoyed night fishing. As a matter of confession, we were known to "rip them off" and tie them to the tips of our rods. Then, whenever a fish was taking our bait, the bells would jingle in the dark and we would excitedly jump to our feet and run to set the hook. The fun we had on the banks of the Ohio was immeasurable. A good fight between an adult catfish and a teenage kid makes for the best of times.

The sound of the bells had a way of making a long wait worth every minute. If we talked at all around the campfire, we kept it to a whisper. We didn't want to miss the tinkling signal. Our ears were carefully tuned to the tips of our rods. Things may be more advanced nowadays in terms of the warning systems for night fishers, but we were proud of our ingenuity.

Give a man a fish
and you feed him for a day.
Teach a man to fish
and you feed him for a lifetime.
PROVERB

Scholars have long known that fishing
eventually turns men into philosophers.
Unfortunately, it is almost impossible to buy
decent tackle on a philosopher's salary.
PATRICK F. MCMANUS

You made him ruler over the works of your hands;
you put everything under his feet:
all flocks and herds,
and the beasts of the field,
the birds of the air,
and the fish of the sea,
all that swim the paths of the seas.

PSALM 8:6-8 NIV

To go fishing is the chance to wash one's soul

with pure air, with the rush of the brook,

or with the shimmer of sun on blue water.

It brings meekness and inspiration

from the decency of nature,

charity toward tackle-makers,

patience toward fish,

a mockery of profits and egos,

a quieting of hate,

a rejoicing that you do not have to decide

a darned thing until next week.

And it is discipline in the equality of men—

for all men are equal before fish.

HERBERT HOOVER

Microwave Ginger Fish

JEAN CHRISTEN

This recipe is an updated version of a traditional Chinese dish where the fish was steamed and typically served with head and tail. You can do the same for this recipe or use fillets. If you use a whole fish, make 3 to 4 diagonal cuts on both sides so the fish will cook properly in the microwave.

Ingredients (Adjust to suit the size of your catch)

1/4 to 1/2 cup light soy sauce
2 to 3 tablespoons rice wine
        (substitute: splash of white wine)
2 to 3 tablespoons shredded ginger
3 to 4 stalks shredded green onions
Cilantro (handful)
1/4 to 1/2 cup vegetable oil

Just as in cooking
there's no such thing
as a little garlic,
in fishing there's
no such thing as a little drag.

H.G. TAPPLY

DIRECTIONS

Rinse the fish and pat dry. Place the fish in a dish deep enough to hold all the ingredients. Sprinkle the fish with wine and soy sauce and 2 to 3 pinches of ginger. Wrap the dish with plastic wrap or cover the dish so it is sealed (we want the fish to steam inside).

Set the microwave on high and cook until the fish is fully cooked—flaky and white to the center. To avoid overcooking the fish, start at 2 to 3 minutes on high and add more minutes as needed. As soon as the fish is cooked, uncover and place cilantro on top.

Quickly heat the oil in a skillet. You'll know it's ready when you see faint smoke/steam rising from the pan. When this happens turn off the burner and toss in the green onions and the rest of the ginger. Stir quickly and then remove the ginger and green onions. (We don't want them to soak up all the oil.) Place the ginger and green onions across the fish and pour the hot, infused oil over the fish from head to tail.

Add more soy sauce to the dish if you like and serve with delicious jasmine rice and stir-fried vegetables. For a delicious and healthy alternative, use brown rice cooked with chicken stock.

Grilled Fish Fillets with Cilantro Lime Butter

LINDSEY WILLIAMS

This delicious recipe works great with tuna, swordfish, wahoo, salmon, red snapper...you name it.
The cilantro lime butter will hook your friends.

Cilantro lime butter
3 tablespoons butter, softened
2 teaspoons freshly grated lime zest
2 tablespoons fresh lime juice
2 small fresh garlic cloves, minced
2 tablespoons minced fresh cilantro leaves

Mix in a small bowl together, and salt and pepper to taste.

Brush fillets (a meaty fish grills best) with olive oil. Lightly salt and pepper the fillets. Grill fish on an oiled rack set 5 to 6 inches above glowing coals until cooked through and firm to the touch.

Top each fillet with a dollop of cilantro lime butter and serve with rice and a fresh garden salad.

For the supreme test of a fisherman
is not how many fish he has caught,
not even how he has caught them,
but what he has caught when he has caught no fish.

JOHN H. BRADLEY

Paul & Andy's Cosmic Marinade and Dressing

BETTY FLETCHER

It doesn't get any easier or more delicious.

Spread a thin layer of mayonnaise and a thin layer of mustard on the surface of the salmon fillet. Add a pinch of sea salt. Bake, skin side down, at 400 degrees for 15 to 20 minutes per inch of thickness.

This marinade/dressing has many uses. Try it with fish, green salads, and pasta dishes.

1/4 cup balsamic vinegar
1/8 cup (2 tablespoons) water
5/8 cup (10 tablespoons) olive oil
1 teaspoon salt
1 to 2 teaspoons Dijon mustard
2 to 6 cloves of garlic, crushed (to taste)

Place all ingredients in shakable container and agitate. (The proportions match those of a Good Seasons dressing bottle. This is a simple way to mix and dispense the marinade.)

Options for use with salmon

Use as marinade for baked salmon. Allow to marinate for at least 2 hours before baking.

Use as a dressing for salmon while barbecuing. Apply liberally during cooking.

Add cooked salmon and steamed vegetables to your favorite pasta and add the marinade to taste for a great pasta salad meal.

Fishing provides that connection with the whole living world. It gives you the opportunity of being totally immersed, turning back into yourself in a good way. A form of meditation, some form of communion with levels of yourself that are deeper than the ordinary self.
TED HUGHES

May the holes in your net
be no larger than the fish in it.
IRISH BLESSING

Mayonnaise Baked Fish with Tropical Salsa

GEORGIA VAROZZA

Slather both sides of fish with mayonnaise and salt and pepper to taste. (Roasted garlic mayonnaise is especially good if you can find it.) Wrap fish loosely in a tinfoil tent and place package on a cookie sheet. Bake fish in 375 degree oven until done. Fish will flake easily when cooked. Do not overcook.

Tropical Salsa
2 papayas, peeled, seeded, and diced small
1/2 green bell pepper, diced small
1/2 red bell pepper, diced small
1/2 red onion, diced small
1 jalapeno pepper, seeded and diced small
1/2 cup fresh cilantro, chopped
juice from one orange
juice from 1 to 2 limes
1 tablespoon cumin
2 teaspoons kosher salt
1 teaspoon black pepper

Mix all ingredients. Keeps in the refrigerator for several days. Serve over baked fish.

Basic Training

UNTIL I MOVED to Tennessee in 1974, my fishing had been limited to throwing a line from the banks of farm ponds and the shores of the Ohio River. I also had some brief experiences with standing in a trout stream and tying myself into knots. Never had I ventured onto the waters in a boat.

In the Nashville area there are two nice lakes. Old Hickory and Percy Priest are a wonderful pair of opportunities for those who enjoy big lake fishing. When I was told that the coves where an angler could find solitude and success were nearly innumerable, I longed to drop a line into them. However, I didn't own a vessel or know anyone who did, so I could only dream about getting out there…until I heard about the rentals at Elm Hill Marina. The idea rolled around in my head for weeks. The one thing that kept me from going straightaway to the marina was not the money. It was the fact that I didn't have a clue how to operate a motorized boat.

Maybe it was the extra strong coffee that day, but one morning I decided to drive out to Percy Priest and make my dreams come true. I went into the office, plopped down my money, signed the papers, and followed the agent down to the dock. Within minutes the motor was puttering in neutral—the agent had started the engine to make sure it was operating well enough for a day's workout. I didn't have a clue how to fire it up.

The fellow stepped out of the boat and said, "Turn the handle counterclockwise to go forward and clockwise to reverse. See you at four this afternoon." With a wave, I climbed in and sat down in front of the engine. I had at least seen enough pictures to know where I was supposed to sit. Other than that, I was at a loss.

My hands shook as I rolled the throttle into reverse. Well…I thought I was putting it into reverse. I had overlooked the fact that when facing forward, one has to think backward to work their hands behind them. "Bang!" Up against the dock I plowed. Quickly I rolled the handle the other way, and I shot across the water like a surface torpedo. I was heading straight for a huge, beautiful sailboat. I jerked the handle sideways and barely missed the hull of the tall boat. Then I heard a scream.

Somehow I had ended up going nearly at full throttle—in reverse—right at a brand-new ski boat. The lady aboard was frantic and her voice screeched, "No! Get away!" Thankfully, I reversed the roll of the throttle, and by the grace of heaven I just missed certain disaster and a probable lawsuit. I ended up back by the dock.

The agent must have heard the commotion because he appeared in a flash. As he approached the dock, he realized he'd rented his boat to a complete novice (a nice way of saying "idiot"). I'll never forget how exasperated he sounded when he threw his cigarette into the water and said, "O.K., step one!" With the skill of a seasoned mariner, in just a few brief moments of instructions on the basics, he had me on my way to the coves I had dreamed about. Though it started with the ingredients for a nightmare, the day turned out quite nice.

To expect to go from an unenlisted sailor straight to the captain's chair is a stunt no swabbie would ever try. How grateful I was for the rental agent's willingness to teach me the basics, and even more grateful that he trusted me to continue on my adventure.

Fishing on the River was not a tame experience. The water was deep. It rushed over huge boulders the size of trucks. It swirled and foamed. If a person fell into it, surviving would be iffy. Consequently, when I was a little shaver, the River terrified me; Dad would move from rock to rock like a mountain goat; but I watched well-back on the bank and prayed fervently that he wouldn't fall into the River. Sometimes I wept out of fear that he would. As I came to respect the danger of the River, but also to enjoy its beauty and be thankful for the trout dinners it furnished, I learned to move from rock to rock like Dad did. Nevertheless, I gave that roaring River its space and didn't tempt it; I never quit watching Dad and other fishing companions to make sure they hadn't slipped and fallen into the River.

HAP LYDA
from *Lyda Lore: A Heritage of Hunting & Fishing, Volume II*

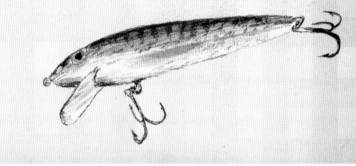

The Heart of a Passion

FISHING AND HUNTING have been longtime winners on our home's list of enjoyable things to do, at least for me and my two children, Nathan and Heidi. My wife, Annie, has never taken to the idea of sitting for hours on a deerstand or handling wiggly nightcrawlers with her bare hands. The kids and I understand her reluctance to venture too far outdoors past her flower garden, but we appreciate her willingness to embrace our adventures.

As it turned out, there was a convenient division of interests that developed among our children when it came to the water and woods. Heidi took to fishing with a passion that would rival Simon Peter and his brother Andrew. Nathan, on the other hand, was our Nimrod—a true hunter. In the middle was a papa who desperately loves to do both. I could not have taken a state-of-the-art computer and engineered a better situation for myself. To have two kids whose affections were so evenly disbursed allowed me to span the entire year in the pleasure of entertaining the joy they each found in the outdoors. What a blessing!

Of all the elements of each activity I wanted to teach them, perhaps one of the most important had to do with attitude more than aptitude. While showing them skills such as casting and shooting was a great deal of fun for me, there was something to be learned that was of greater import. I wanted them to deeply respect the life of the creatures we would capture and consume. To go to a deerstand or a lake without regard for the blood that flowed through the veins of an animal or a fish was not allowed. There had to be an understanding that while we as humans have dominion over all that flies, crawls, or swims, these creatures do have feelings.

I managed to teach Nathan and Heidi that shedding the blood of the game had to be accompanied by a certain remorse. Without it, we would merely be murderers. I realize there seems to be a great conflict between these two ideas. But believing that mankind has a right to "harvest" the fish, furry animals, and birds for food means we are not restricted from the pursuit. While we admittedly enjoy the challenge of developing and using the skills required to outsmart our prey, we cannot come to the moment of taking their lives with a casual spirit.

Many nights following a kill earlier in the day, I have laid my head on my pillow and been unable to fall quickly to sleep. I know it sounds odd, but I am invariably haunted by the sight of a creature that has died at my hands. I can only hope that my children will carry this strange irony of the heart through their hunting and fishing years.

It has always been my private conviction
that any man who pits
his intelligence against a fish and loses
has it coming.
JOHN STEINBECK

Three-fourths of the Earth's surface
is water and one-fourth is land.
It ... e clear that the good Lord intended
... spend triple the amount of time

All in the Wrist

One of my favorite parts of the fishing routine is casting. There is something in my psyche that allows me to feel very satisfied when I see my bait splash a mere inch or two from where I wanted it to fall. To know my eye/hand coordination is working well is most rewarding. If all I got done at the lake was a good day of accurate casting, I could go home with no reason to complain. Hooking a fish, of course, takes the joy to the next level, but I refuse to complain if it doesn't happen.

Luck affects everything.

Let your hook always be cast;

in the stream where you least expect it

there will be a fish.

Ovid

They took their way towards the house

on the opposite side of the river,

in the nearest direction;

but their progress was slow, for Mr. Gardiner,

though seldom able to indulge the taste,

was very fond of fishing,

and was so much engaged in watching the

occasional appearance of some trout in the water,

and talking to the man about them,

that he advanced but little.

Jane Austen, *Pride and Prejudice*

OLD VESSELS

SADNESS WASHED OVER ME when I saw it sitting in our neighbor's backyard. The old fishing boat had been there when we first moved in the summer of 1988, and it was still in the same spot when we moved away in 1996. I'm not sure how long it sat in the yard before we arrived, but the sight of it tore at me each time I took it in.

The craft was an olive-green aluminum boat. As a result of its long stay in the shadows of the trees, it was covered with sap and mildew. The many spring seasons had brought new crops of leaves and many autumns dumped them into the unused boat. The flat tires of the trailer were buried in the dirt, and grass had overtaken the axles. What a pitiful scene it was.

We were unable to get to know the owners of the boat. We knew their names and a few other items about them, but that was about it. As far as their relationship with their lonely boat was concerned, I assumed it was a "toy" the family had enjoyed for a while. I couldn't be sure. But one thing was for certain, there was a day when they brought it home

Pop and Don were great teachers, helping me cast, instructing me about angles. But the biggest lesson they taught me was patience. When I saw that bite, I'd automatically want to start reeling in. But there's an art to landing a fish.

MIKE IACONELLI
from *Fishing on the Edge*

Good fishing never stops.
There are only times when in some
places it is better than others.

GEORGE FICHTER

from the marine dealer and proudly parked it in their yard. They probably even peeked through the window blinds that evening and dreamed of the fun it represented.

I also suspect there was good care given at first to the old boat. A cleaning cloth probably slid faithfully across its hull after it was retrailered and brought back home from the lake. The carpet was likely vacuumed. The drain plug was pulled so it would empty of residual water. The required maintenance was done to keep the small outboard motor in good running order. The prized possession was likely treated as one of the family until one day something began to change. Perhaps the kids grew up and their interest in going fishing waned. As a result, the boat sat longer and longer between trips to the water. Maybe the dad got too busy maintaining a living. At some unknown point in time there was a lifelessness about the boat out back that became unnoticed.

Admitting there is still enough "little kid" left in me to humanize inanimate things, I imagined the old fishing boat might have had something to say about its sad state. Feeling quite lonely, it may have wakened and spoke each time it heard our neighbor's lawn mower start up. "Ah ha! They're mowing the yard today. Maybe they'll see me and pull me out of this mud hole to take me to the lake. There I'll see friends I haven't seen for so long. And, oh, how I long to feel the water flowing across my belly again. Perhaps today!" But it wasn't to be. Day after day, summer after summer, year after year the time passed until the old boat was completely forgotten. Ignored by its family, it

> The charm of fishing is that it is the pursuit of what is elusive but attainable, a perpetual series of occasions for hope.
> JOHN BUCHAN

lowered its bow one evening and died.

When I came along, what I saw was not just an old, dilapidated, aluminum boat. It was a haunting reminder of some folks I've seen in my day. At one time they were valued and felt a usefulness that kept them energized and shipshape. Then somewhere along the path of time, they were forgotten. Others around them got distracted by life. Eventually they were left only with hope that people would come along, find them worthy of their attention, and give them a home where they would be loved and appreciated.

Most of us do not have to look very far to find an "old vessel" whose spirit is barely alive. They are around us, some right in our own homes. Perhaps it's time to go to them and see if they can be encouraged.

For one thing—as the salmon fishers tell it— either you catch a fish way too soon, before you're fully able to appreciate it, or you have to wait much longer than you think you should have to, so that when you finally hook and land one the elation is tempered by a profound sense of relief. And, of course, repeated failures don't lead you to the logical conclusion; they only whet your appetite.

JOHN GIERACH *Dances with Trout*

O the gallant Fisher's life,
It is the best of any;
'Tis full of, void of strife,
And 'tis be pleasure, loved of many:
Other joys
Are but toys;
Only this
Lawful is;
For our skill
Breeds no ill,
But content and pleasure.

IZAAK WALTON
The Compleat Angler

But for me, as it had been for my father and grandfather, fishing was a necessity, though why I love it and continue to pursue it with such passion is as mysterious and beguiling as the black water in that North Carolina farm pond.

MONTE BURKE

from the preface of *Sowbelly*

There's a fine line between fishing and standing on the shore like an idiot.
STEVE WRIGHT

ON THE LINE

AS A KID GROWING UP in West Virginia, one of the highlights of the year was the annual church fundraiser fair. The room was filled with tables and booths that featured crafts, homemade pies, and other items. All the goodies were designed to capture the cash in the purses and wallets of those who filed through. It was always a successful event.

It was at the fair that I was introduced to an emotion that I still enjoy to this day—so much so that I make time and financial sacrifices to experience it. It happened at the fishing booth. It was a corner area simply equipped and usually manned by two individuals. Separating them from the crowd was a tall curtain made from a few bed sheets hung over a strand of clothesline that stretched from one wall to another. The divider that was created spanned approximately ten feet in width and seven feet in height.

The "fish" the children would catch was a brown paper bag that was attached to the twine by a hook made out of a clothespin. In the sack was a plastic trinket. For me, this was not the real prize. As it turned out, the trophy I landed that first time I went "curtain fishing" is mounted on the wall of my heart. It was the excitement of feeling the tug on the pole when the person hidden behind the cloth would give the line a couple of quick jerks to let me know it was time to reel in my catch.

The tug didn't happen immediately after I cast the twine over the drapery. Because the person behind it had to take a moment to attach the bag to the hook, there was a delay that allowed enough time to let some tension build in my mind. The anticipation was sweet. I could hardly hold still.

Suddenly it happened! I'll never forget the feeling the first time that bamboo pole danced in my hands. There was something mysterious about being connected to the unseen. To know that evidence of its existence had presented itself, and that I would soon be able to see it, was more excitement than a little boy should have been allowed to experience. My heart pounded with joy as if I had hooked a blue marlin off the coast of Florida!

Today, whenever I go fishing, the one thing I look forward to the most is that telltale tug on the line.

James Hautman

WE SURFCASTERS assume that as in life, the big fish are just beyond our reach, which usually is not the case. Bass, in fact, cruise so close to the shore they often resist lunging at a lure until the final few yards of a retrieve. And even if they all spurn my plug, sensing it's indeed a fake fish, this doesn't stop me from going out again the next day.

Of course, the thrill of marching home with a fat bluefish or gorgeous striper in hand is not to be lightly dismissed. The hunter's triumphant return is a familiar scene in history, recorded all the way back in the earliest cave paintings. But for me bringing home a fish is simply a bonus. The solitude of surfcasting is my main enjoyment— to be savored like a fine wine or a fragrant flower.

ROY ROWAN, *Surfcaster's Quest*

There is certainly something
in angling that tends to produce
a serenity of the mind.

WASHINGTON IRVING

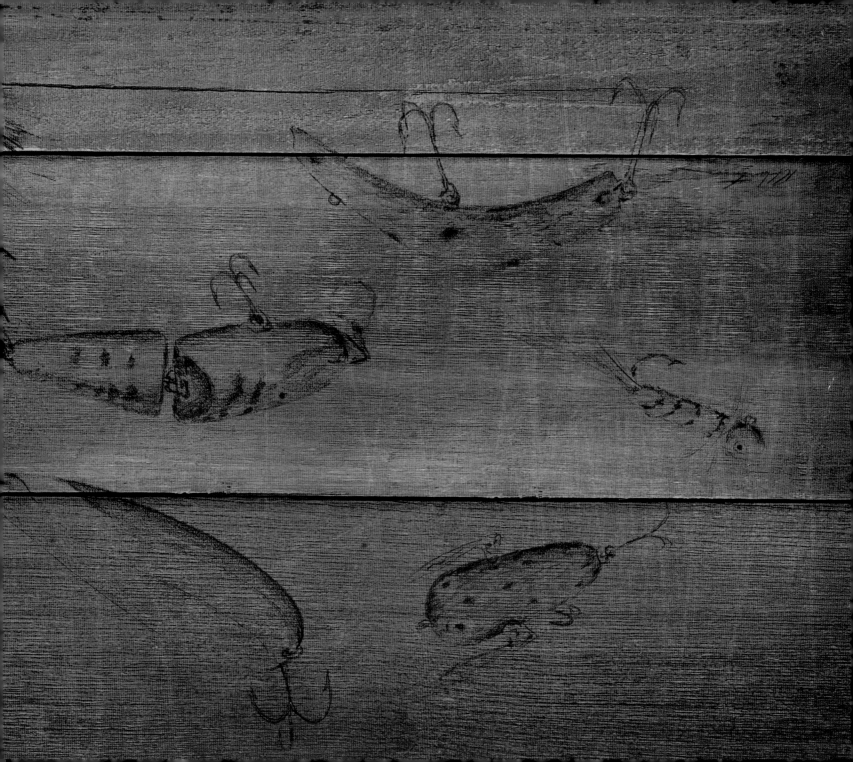

Princess Puffybottom

...AND DARRYL

Written by

Susin Nielsen

Illustrated by

Olivia Chin Mueller

tundra

Princess Puffybottom

had the perfect life.

Her subjects served her delicious meals.

If they were late,
she gave them a firm
but gentle reminder.

They also took care of more delicate matters.

In return, Princess Puffybottom
permitted some petting.

And she humored them once in a while.

Life was good.

Until the day Darryl arrived.

He was horrible.

He was disgusting.

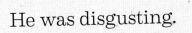

He was an *animal!*

Princess Puffybottom knew he would not last.

Darryl would be banished.

It was only a matter of time.

So she waited.

And waited.

And waited.

Finally, the day arrived.
Her subjects left with Darryl,
and they were gone
for a very long time.

Princess Puffybottom celebrated.

She knew that they were taking him to a faraway kingdom.

Her subjects eventually returned . . .

With Darryl.

Princess Puffybottom was not amused.
Princess Puffybottom knew that
something had to be done.

Nothing worked.
Darryl was here to stay.

Princess Puffybottom was sad.

Nobody seemed to notice . . .

except Darryl.

He was very annoying. He followed her everywhere.

Darryl was not bright.
Darryl was not
sophisticated . . .

But he had his uses.

And Darryl worshipped her.

He put her on a pedestal.

So Princess Puffybottom tolerated Darryl . . .

most of the time.

Life was good again.

At least her subjects wouldn't be bringing
home any more surprises.

To T.W. — for believing in me, and for
your ability to always (kindly) challenge
me to do better. You may be a dog person,
but I still adore you. — S.N.

For Minnow,
my own puffy-bottomed cat!
— O.C.M.

Tundra Books, an imprint of Penguin Random House Canada Young Readers,
a Penguin Random House Company

Library and Archives Canada Cataloguing in Publication

Nielsen, Susin, 1964-, author
     Princess Puffybottom . . . and Darryl / Susin Nielsen ; illustrated by
Olivia Chin Mueller.

Issued in print and electronic formats.
ISBN 978-1-101-91925-5 (hardcover).—ISBN 978-1-101-91926-2 (EPUB)

     I. Mueller, Olivia Chin, illustrator II. Title.

PS8577.I37P75 2019   jC813'.54   C2017-902912-6
                                               C2017-902913-4

Published simultaneously in the United States of America by Tundra Books of Northern New York,
an imprint of Penguin Random House Canada Young Readers, a Penguin Random House Company

Library of Congress Control Number: 2017940268

Edited by Tara Walker
Designed by Kelly Hill
The artwork in this book was created digitally.
The text was set in Eames Century Modern.

Printed and bound in China

www.penguinrandomhouse.ca

1 2 3 4 5   23 22 21 20 19

Penguin
Random House
TUNDRA BOOKS